The EUCHARIST

50 QUESTIONS *From the* PEWS

Richard N. Fragomeni, PhD

D0061564

Liguori
LIGUORI, MISSOURI

Imprimi Potest:
Thomas D. Picton, C.Ss.R.
Provincial, Denver Province
The Redemptorists

"In accordance with *Code of Canon Law,* c. 827, permission to publish has been granted on December 9, 2008 by the Very Reverend John F. Canary, Vicar General, Archdiocese of Chicago. Permission to publish is an indication that nothing contrary to Church teaching is contained in this work. It does not imply any endorsement of the opinions expressed in the publication; nor is any liability assumed by this permission."—By the Archdiocese of Chicago.

Published by Liguori Publications
Liguori, Missouri 63057-9999

Library of Congress Cataloging-in-Publication Data

Fragomeni, Richard N.
    The Eucharist / Richard Fragomeni.
      p. cm.
    ISBN 978-0-7648-1699-4
    1. Lord's Supper–Catholic Church–Miscellanea. 2. Catholic Church–Doctrines–Miscellanea. I. Title.
    BX2215.3. F73 2008
    264'.02036–dc22

                                 2008045020

Liguori Publications, a nonprofit corporation, is an apostolate of the Redemptorists. To learn more about the Redemptorists, visit Redemptorists.com.

To order, call 800-325-9521
www.liguori.org

Printed in the United States of America
12 11 10 09 08   5 4 3 2 1
First edition

TABLE OF CONTENTS

Part III: Theological Questions • 43

Part IV: Pastoral Questions • 73

INTRODUCTION

Religious practices are a kind of language, a way of communicating something important. The celebration of the liturgical rites, especially the Eucharist, is a great symphony of gestures, signs, symbols, words, and relationships. Devotional practices are also a language. They can communicate a profound personal longing for God that official liturgical practices don't always address adequately.

Since the Second Vatican Council, Catholics have been invited by Church leadership to engage in a spiritual renewal that finds its source and summit in the celebration of the liturgy, especially the Eucharist. Devotional prayer is one aspect of the Church's renewal that has gained momentum, reviving rites and rituals that are new and unknown to many. The people in the pews have many questions about them.

The fifty questions in this booklet were raised by people from several midwestern parishes. The editors of Liguori Publications surfaced these questions as a way of giving voice to the concerns of laypeople interested in understanding what we do in prayer and how the Eucharist and eucharistic devotions form the core of the spiritual renewal of the baptized community. In answering these questions, I used pastoral experience, Church documents, and common sense. A complete list of sources begins on page 91.

I hope my answers prompt further thinking about the questions, perhaps even dialogue with others who have interest in the Eucharist. I also hope that by understanding the eucharistic and devotional practices addressed by these questions, people will have a fuller and richer participation in the mystery of Christ and the Spirit at the heart of all prayer. Understanding what we do *as we do it* creates rich insight. Such attentive awareness allows God's voice to speak in the language of our lives and hearts.

RICHARD N. FRAGOMENI, PHD
AUGUST 1, 2008
THE FEAST OF SAINT ALPHONSUS LIGUORI

Part I

DEVOTIONAL QUESTIONS

1. What is spiritual communion?

Spiritual communion is a unique Roman Catholic devotional practice not to be confused with *sacramental* Communion, the participation in the mystery of Christ by eating and drinking the Body and the Blood of the Lord.

The development of spiritual communion as a devotion can be traced to Saint Alphonsus Liguori. Basically, it's a form of spiritual yearning to be in communion with Christ during those times when his sacramental gift cannot be shared.

To share in sacramental communion, one must be aware of no unconfessed serious sin against God's commands and be in good standing with the Roman Catholic Church. With exceptions for age and health, one must also have fasted from all food and all beverages except water for one hour before receiving sacramental Communion (also see question 46).

Some Catholics are unable to share sacramental Communion because of sickness, geographic distance from a Roman Catholic community, or unavailability of priests.

Any Christian who wishes to have spiritual communion with the Lord can do so by taking a moment to consider God's love demonstrated to us in the life, passion, and death of Christ. Give thanks to God for this wonderful gift, and say a prayer of spiritual communion such as this one written by Saint Alphonsus Liguori:

> My Jesus, I believe you are really here
> in the Blessed Sacrament.
> I love you more than anything in the world,
> and I hunger to receive you.
> But since I cannot receive Communion at this
> moment, feed my soul at least spiritually.
> I unite myself to you now as I do
> when I actually receive you.
> Never let me drift away from you.

FROM *VISITS TO JESUS AND MARY*
© 2006 LIGUORI PUBLICATIONS

---

2. What is the symbolic relationship between the altar and the Eucharist?

The altar, also called the table of the Lord, is not just a piece of furniture. Our early Christian ancestors gathered at dining-room tables for the Eucharist, and through the centuries that simple piece of furniture came alive with deep meanings we still cherish.

It is from the altar that we share in the Eucharist, and the altar resonates with the presence of Christ. The altar is consecrated by a bishop and anointed with chrism just as Christ was anointed priest, prophet, and king. In many places, the altar also contains the relics of martyrs and saints.

The gestures and rituals of the Roman Catholic Church express the sentiments of our faith and our hearts. We bow and genuflect to express reverence, honor, and devotion. These gestures are used not only by Roman Catholics and other Christians, but by various other people of faith, including Jews, Muslims, and Buddhists.

After the consecrated host and chalice are raised and shown to the assembly by the priest, he genuflects, and any concelebrants bow to the host and chalice. Norms exist for bowing to the altar and, at some points of the eucharistic celebration, kissing the altar. The kiss is a more intimate act of showing reverence and honor.

The altar is a tangible sign of Christ. We bow to the altar during the eucharistic liturgy and outside of the Mass as well, because for Roman Catholics it's the central place of our encounter with Christ and with the great communion of saints.

---

3. **My church has many Spanish traditions, one of which is the procession. Why are processions important, and why don't more churches have them?**

The *procession* is an ancient form of prayer found in most religions. Some psalms from the Jewish tradition speak about processing to the Temple. In fact, Psalm 43:4 is used in the Latin Mass during the prayers at the foot of the altar.

Processions are like mini-pilgrimages in that they are all about moving toward a sanctuary or shrine where God can be encountered. But while pilgrimages usually move long distances and take many days to reach the sacred destination, a procession is much shorter and can be completed without considering lodging, food, or provisions.

From a broader viewpoint, movement toward a holy destination in a procession or pilgrimage can be understood as a metaphor for life itself. Life is a journey, a pilgrimage, a procession. Some would say we are all in a procession to the grave. This is true, but the religious perspective adds a dimension to this destination. Christians believe our procession through life leads ultimately to the New Jerusalem, the place in God's heaven where there will be no more death, no more fear, no more suffering. It's a destination that will bring us the fullness of life and lead us to see God as God is. At funerals, Eucharistic Prayer III adds that on that day we'll become like God and praise God forever.

Throughout the liturgical year, the Roman Catholic community is given many opportunities to have processions. At each weekly Eucharist, the procession of the assembly to share the Communion gift proclaims our hope of full communion with all creation in the New World of God's peace. On the feast of the Presentation of the Lord (February 2), a procession of candles moves from one location into the church building. This procession celebrates and commemorates the entrance of light into the Temple forty days after Christmas.

Another great moment of movement is on Palm Sunday. The solemn blessing and procession, in which the community carries palms and sings "Hosanna in the highest" or another antiphon, is the formal journey into the beginning of Holy Week. And certainly the procession with the Blessed Sacrament on the solemnity of The Most Holy Body and Blood of Christ (*Corpus Christi*) brings the movement of prayer around neighborhoods and cities as we bless and pray for all who journey together in a given locale.

Processions are part of the religious heritage of Roman Catholics. Certain cultural groups, like the Hispanic community in the United States, keep this form of prayer alive. Many parish communities are beginning to understand the rich value of processions and are incorporating them into the life of the parish communities.

4. What's the difference between the Sacred Heart of Jesus and the Eucharistic Heart of Jesus?

There is no difference. Both titles get at the same reality: the Heart of Christ is brimming with compassion, mercy, and love for all persons and for all creation.

Devotion to the Heart of Christ grew up a few centuries ago in Europe, when many Roman Catholics thought God/Christ was a punitive force out to condemn and destroy sinners. There was a sense that we are worth to God only what our actions dictate, and the fear, scrupulosity, and self-loathing that entered the Christian imagination became an exaggerated paranoia that caused people to live in guilt, shame, and despair.

The devotion to the Heart of Christ was a grassroots movement to correct this error. Made most popular by the visions and writings of Saint Margaret Mary Alacoque, a French

Visitation nun (1647–1690), the devotion blossomed. It was an invitation to open one's heart to trusting in the love of Christ, who was not out to get us, but to embrace us in mercy. A devotee would celebrate the sacrament of reconciliation, share in the gift of holy Communion, pray for the intentions of the Church for nine consecutive first Fridays, and be given, by the promise of Christ to Saint Margaret Mary, the hope of peaceful death and the mercy of God.

Devotion to the Heart of Christ continues today in a renewed way with the devotion to Divine Mercy. Inaugurated by a visionary Polish nun, Saint Mary Faustina Kowalska (1905–1938; Congregation of the Sisters of Our Lady of Mercy), the devotion to Divine Mercy centers upon the prayer to the Heart of Christ. As the portrait of Divine Mercy illustrates, the Heart of Christ is filled with red and white rays of light shining on sinners who invoke mercy upon themselves and upon the whole world. This prayer, called the *Divine Mercy chaplet,* is usually prayed in front of the Blessed Sacrament solemnly enthroned upon the altar in a *monstrance,* a large container typically shaped like a large sunburst. Thus we can see how the image of the eucharistic Heart of Jesus is understood.

Regardless of which image is used, devotion to the Heart of Christ is a key that allows Roman Catholics access to the treasure of God's mercy.

5. What is benediction?

The word *benediction* has several meanings. The first type of benediction is a prayer for blessing, that is, an invocation of God's power and light upon a person or object. For instance, the prayer spoken before a meal or before a gathering of people who seek the guidance and blessings of God is called a benediction. A benediction is also sometimes bestowed upon a religious object like a rosary. The *Book of Blessings* gives benedictions for various other circumstances, like the blessing of a library or over animals. It's noted in the *Book of Blessings* that laypeople may do benedictions on certain occasions, for example, the blessing of throats in commemoration of Saint Blaise.

The second type of benediction is the *Benediction of the Blessed Sacrament*, the solemn blessing of an assembly of believers with the eucharistic bread. This devotion, present in the Western Catholic Church since the Middle Ages, continues today as a popular form of prayer and invocation of Christ's blessing. Placed within the context of a prayer service, including song, the reading of Scripture, preaching, and silent prayer, Benediction of the Blessed Sacrament is a devotional activity to be performed only by an ordained priest or deacon.

The eucharistic bread is reserved in a tabernacle, usually in a special container called a *pyx*. The pyx is placed in a *monstrance* or *ostensorium*, a large container usually made of precious metals and jewels and typically shaped like a large sunburst. The consecrated host is placed at the center of the sunburst in a glass chamber that allows the host to be seen.

The priest wears a ceremonial shawl called a *humeral veil*.

At the close of the prayer service, he takes the monstrance into his veiled hands, faces the assembly, and blesses the people by making the Sign of the Cross with the monstrance. During the blessing, the people usually make the Sign of the Cross as a way of accepting and receiving the blessings of Christ. On more solemn occasions, this Benediction is accompanied by the ringing of bells and the swinging of incense to demonstrate honor and praise.

The devotional practice of benediction in all its forms is a Roman Catholic tradition that invokes the power of God upon people. The people who are blessed are then sent into the world to be a benediction for others in the ways of peace and justice.

6. What is the difference between Benediction of the Blessed Sacrament and Exposition of the Eucharist?

Exposition and Benediction are the beginning and ending rituals of adoration of the Eucharist, a devotion which has been observed for many centuries in the Roman Catholic Church. In Exposition, the Blessed Sacrament is placed in a monstrance so that public adoration of the Eucharist can take place. In Benediction of the Blessed Sacrament (see question 5), the priest or deacon blesses the assembly with the consecrated host.

Designated laypersons can do the Exposition of the Eucharist, but Benediction of the Blessed Sacrament can be performed only by a priest or deacon. A layperson may return the Eucharist to the tabernacle after adoration.

Originally, the consecrated bread was reserved in homes

and churches primarily for sharing Communion outside Mass with the sick and dying. It wasn't until the Middle Ages that adoration of the Eucharist exposed in a monstrance or simply locked in a tabernacle became an important devotion. Eventually, communities of religious women were established to perpetually adore the Eucharist as an act of reparation and love to Christ, so wounded by the sins of the people.

At the encouragement of Pope John Paul II, adoration of the Eucharist has increased in popularity. Parishes throughout the United States have perpetual-adoration societies and chapels where the Eucharist is exposed twenty-four hours a day.

The devotion of adoration of the Eucharist can be a time of great stillness for those who practice it. It is never to be a substitute for the celebration of the Eucharist or the reception of holy Communion, but adoration as a form of prayer, meditation, and contemplation is a valuable source of openness to Christ, who speaks to us in the silence.

7. Why is a lighted candle always in front of the tabernacle in my church?

The 2002 *General Instruction of the Roman Missal* states that a lamp should be kept burning near the tabernacle to show and honor the Real Presence of Christ in the tabernacle. In the past, this candle was to be made of fine-quality beeswax. Now it can be fueled by either wax or oil, with no specification of the kind or quality (paragraph 316).

This use of a candle or oil lamp is not new to Christianity. We see the use of lamps near the Holy of Holies, a room in the Temple of Jerusalem. The vision of the heavenly throne room, portrayed vividly in the Book of Daniel, describes the use of lamps in front of the divine throne. In our own day, a perpetual flame honors the dead at the graves of the Unknown Soldier and President John F. Kennedy.

Some pastors ask parishioners to help purchase these candles and lamps. In return, these lamps are lighted for the intentions of donors, making these candles also acts of petition before the reserved Eucharist.

8. When and where did perpetual adoration develop?

Adoration of the Eucharist can be traced to the early centuries of western Christianity, but the actual practice of perpetually adoring the Eucharist began most clearly in Europe after the Council of Trent (1545–1563).

Evidence exists that an Austrian community of cloistered Benedictine nuns took vows of perpetual adoration in the seventeenth century. As the number of cloistered communities dedicated to perpetual adoration grew throughout Europe, the need also arose to bring this devotion to the laity. By the nineteenth century, various practices of adoration of the Eucharist were established.

By the mid-nineteenth century, French Saint Pierre-Julien Eymard started the Congregation of the Blessed Sacrament for men to instill in the lay faithful the desire to honor and worship Christ in the Eucharist. Saint Pierre-Julien built churches dedicated to perpetual adoration and inspired many to make a holy hour in the presence of the Blessed Sacrament.

By the mid-twentieth century, the practice of perpetual

adoration began to fade away. With the renewal of the liturgy and the accent on the baptismal priesthood's role of justice in the modern world, many types of devotional practices waned, including devotion to visiting the Blessed Sacrament.

Pope John Paul II, however, revised the practice of perpetual adoration, and today parishes throughout the United States have special chapels in which parishioners are encouraged to spend at least one hour a week in adoration. Pious societies promote perpetual adoration as a way of giving praise and thanks to Christ and as a place to ask for intercession for those in peril or raising questions about life and death.

Some have suggested the practice of perpetual adoration should be linked to the corporal and spiritual works of mercy. Parishioners could pray for an hour in the stillness of the living presence of Christ and then perform an hour of service in the parish or diocese, thus touching Christ where he said he would be found: in the hungry, the thirsty, the needy, the sick, and the imprisoned.

Part II

LITURGICAL QUESTIONS

9. Why must we fast before receiving the Eucharist?

Fasting, an ancient spiritual exercise in which one refrains from food and drink during a designated period of time, is practiced by religious people around the world for a variety of reasons. For example, during the days of Ramadan, followers of Muhammad (Muslims) fast from sunrise to sunset to purify the mind and body. Buddhist monks have fasted publicly as a protest to injustice.

Catholics also fast, most significantly during the Lenten season and before receiving the Eucharist. During Lent, we fast to show solidarity with catechumens preparing for the sacraments of initiation as well as with Christ, who fasted in the desert. We also pray and give alms during Lent. In addition, the fast from food and drink before Communion can create a physical hunger that becomes a sign of the spiritual hunger only God can fill, a tangible grumbling of the body that signals the spiritual groaning of the heart to find our satisfaction in Christ.

These practices are not an attempt to win God's favor, but to create space in a person for the action of God to work in us. Lenten fasting isn't just about food. One can also fast from parts of one's life that may get too cluttered to let God in. Some fast from prejudice of all kinds, from excessive use of the media and Internet, and from certain entertainments. This wider understanding of fasting resonates with the motive of making space for God to enter. When God enters, everything can be changed. And isn't that what Lent is really all about, being changed into the image and likeness of the Risen Lord?

Currently, Catholics are asked to fast from food and all beverages but water for one hour before receiving the Eucharist. In the past, the eucharistic fast lasted three hours before Communion. For many centuries before that, the fast was from midnight until the morning reception of the sacrament.

These varied time limits reflect different customs of fasting, but all acknowledge the same religious sentiment. The physical hunger was probably better felt when we fasted from midnight, so even though the current requirement is only an hour, there is no reason we can't practice a longer period of fasting before Communion as a spiritual discipline of preparation for the gift of the Eucharist.

10. Why are we not allowed to receive the Eucharist more than once a day?

Actually, we are.

After the Second Vatican Council (1962–1965), the Roman Catholic Church reinstated an ancient practice of calculating the beginning of a day not at midnight, but in the evening. As a result, Saturday-evening celebrations of the Sunday Eucharist were introduced around the world. People asked whether they could receive the Eucharist at Mass on Saturday morning and again on Saturday night, and the Roman authorities said yes. They also said that if we went to Mass the next morning, we could share in holy Communion even though technically we had already received Sunday Eucharist the night before.

The same is true at Christmas. If you share in the Eucharist at midnight Mass and then attend dawn Mass, you may share in the Eucharist a second time.

These pastoral practices caused a change to canon law 917. The revised code, in fact, encourages a more universal invitation to Communion whenever a Catholic participates in a eucharistic celebration on any day of the year.

Two words of caution: first, it is a real gift to share frequently in the Eucharist—after all, many Catholics are denied Communion for long periods of time because of the priest shortage—and we shouldn't take it for granted. Second, we must be sure the frequent reception of the Eucharist doesn't turn into a religious fetish or some kind of magical practice. We must be mindful that what we are given to receive is what we are also called to become: the Living Body of Christ, transformed in grace to love and serve the Lord.

11. Why does the homily last longer than the time for private reflection after holy Communion?

Silence is becoming extinct. In many places in the world, noise pollution gets in the way of one of the most essential human needs: depth of soul, which is available only through the doorway of silence, the stillness of the inner and outer world.

Many opportunities for silence exist during the liturgy:

- Before Mass begins
- At the penitential rite
- Before the opening prayer
- After the first reading and before the responsorial psalm
- After the second reading and before the Gospel acclamation
- After the homily
- After the community has shared the Eucharist

Like silence in the larger human experience, however, these moments in liturgy are also becoming extinct. People who celebrate the Latin Mass say one of its appeals is the amount of silence. The reality, however, is that the same silence is afforded those who celebrate the ordinary form of the Roman rite—we just don't seem to take advantage of those moments. For example, silence is called for before Mass begins, but it's a very difficult silence to negotiate, especially in communities where the Sunday celebration is a lively gathering of friends.

Here are a few considerations: First, the problem of silence cannot be easily handled in the liturgy if it is not being handled in human life. Silence is a discipline that must be practiced. This is a matter of formation that could be instilled in children at Catholic school and in religious-education classes. Parents should be encouraged to cultivate times of silence at home.

Second, catechesis about silence could easily be part of a parish plan for adult education. While it is not responsible for a priest to make the homily an instruction, the priest can shape and form awareness about silence in a series of bulletin announcements or in a series of short presentations about silence before the Sunday celebration begins.

Finally, when all is said and done, the best way to catechize about silence is to do it. Recently a high-ranking bishop celebrated the Eucharist. After Communion was given, the music over, the vessels cleaned, and the ministers in their places, the bishop sat in silence. After a few moments of initial flutter by the assembly, the silence took over, and a great stillness happened. In that silence, the angels sang.

---

12. Why do some churches use bells during the consecration and others do not?

We ring bells because they make a beautiful sound for the Lord and for our ears as well. They signal something important, they bring us comfort in sorrow, and they double our joy.

The official name for the ringing of the bells is *tintinnabulation*. As with so many practices, tintinnabulation is present in many cultural and religious traditions around the globe. It is a beautiful way to focus the mind and the heart. It is a wonderful way to lift the soul to God.

A few years ago, I was in Assisi for Holy Week and the Easter Triduum. The liturgy and popular devotions will always be etched in my heart. The community of faith, the singing, the preaching, and the pageantry were all meaningful.

But what I remember most vividly about those days is the sunrise tintinnabulation on Easter Sunday. Imagine being up half the night at the Easter Vigil. Then at dawn, you hear literally all the bells in Assisi begin to ring—*all* the bells, which seems like hundreds. The bells sounded for fifteen minutes. I had never heard anything so beautiful. The tintinnabulation stirred my soul. It was the resurrection song, loud and clear, silver-toned and full of exuberant new life. Needless to say, I did not go back to sleep that morning. I was up and ready for the early-morning celebration at the Basilica of Saint Francis.

Catholics ring bells at the Eucharist, during the singing of the Gloria on Holy Thursday and at the Easter Vigil, at the showing of the consecrated bread and wine and, in some places, at the beginning of the preparation of the gifts and the Communion procession. We also ring bells to mark the morning, noon, and evening hours, at which times devotion takes us into the memory of the Incarnation of Christ and the praying of the Angelus. Bells are rung to assemble the community for prayer and festivities. At weddings and funerals, bells declare that something important is happening—an event that must be surrounded by a beautiful sound.

But why do some churches use bells during the consecration and others do not? The books of the revised liturgy give an option, so some parish leaders choose to ring bells and others do not. However, in the Latin Mass, there is no option—the bells must be rung at set times.

On that Easter morning in Assisi, I "got it" about ringing bells. I had understood in my head what I was taught about bell-ringing in the Catholic tradition, but that Easter I got it in my heart. I began encouraging parish leaders to ring bells whenever the liturgy allows. I suggest the bells be of fine quality and musically pleasing to the ear. Personally, I don't think it's a custom we should lose, because it's a holy sound that can cause the heart to rejoice. Tintinnabulation links us to God.

---

13. Why doesn't the host look, feel, or taste like bread?

It should. Catholics believe that on the night before Jesus died, he had one last supper with his disciples. During that meal, "he broke [the bread] and gave it to them, saying, 'This is my body, which is given for you. Do this in remembrance of me.' And he did the same with the cup after supper, saying, 'This cup that is poured out for you is the new covenant in my blood' " (Luke 22:19–20). From this narrative, it is clear that bread and wine were shared by Christ with the disciples and, through the Tradition, are also shared with us.

It seems clear from history that the wine used at the time of Jesus was made from grapes. Most likely, then, Jesus used grape wine on the night he was betrayed. It's not that clear, however, what the bread was made from. Since our hosts today are made from wheat flour, we assume that's what Jesus' bread was made from. Yet some contemporary scholars believe Jesus used unleavened loaves of bread made from barley flour because Jesus' last meal took place during Passover, a feast associated with the barley harvest.

For nearly eight hundred years, the Western Catholic

Church used leavened wheat bread for the Eucharist, most likely because it was the bread used by the people of the times and therefore was most readily available. The use of leavened wheat bread continues in both the Eastern rite Catholic communities and the Orthodox Churches.

Why did the change to unleavened wheat bread occur in the West? Several factors seem to intersect. Scholars suggest that around the ninth century, the Western Church became more and more interested in the cultic dimensions of the liturgy and looked for ways to accent the continuity of the Eucharist with Christ. Since it was believed that Christ used unleavened wheat bread, that's what was introduced into the Roman rite. By the beginning of the new millennium, devotions such as exposition and adoration of the eucharistic Bread had developed. Unleavened bread doesn't mold and can be more easily kept and exposed without spoiling, so it was better suited for use in the devotions than leavened bread.

But can unleavened bread ever feel, look, or taste like leavened bread? The Second Vatican Council (1962–1965) called for a renewal of the sacramental and liturgical life of the Church and for the fullness of signs and symbols to be highly valued and reinstated in the Roman rite. This directive echoes an ancient sacramental principle: the more authentic the elements of the sacrament, the more authentic the sacramental experience. This is why we began to see immersion pools for baptism and a rich use of water and oil during these rites. The community is once again given the fullness of the sign of Communion by being offered the Cup of Salvation in addition to the Bread of Life. Richer use of the basic elements of bread, wine, water, and oil is meant to deepen the sacramental experience and the openness of the community to the grace of Christ and the Spirit.

The problem is that it's difficult to make a rich sign of the bread if it must be unleavened and made only of flour and water. Some have commented that it takes more faith to believe the host is bread than to believe it's the Body of Christ.

Many parishes tried to keep to the letter *and* spirit of the law by creating bread with nonleavening additives that gave it substance, color, and form. However, those experiments have since been prohibited. Some parishes buy hosts from convents that manufacture larger, more substantial hosts. This seems to be the best way to handle the tension between the letter of the law and the spirit of a renewed liturgy.

14. Is it permissible for the Eucharist to be given in the hand to someone wearing gloves?

For centuries, baptized Catholics were allowed to receive the Eucharist only on their tongues, usually while kneeling. But texts dating from the fourth century tell us that early Christians received the Eucharist in their hands. Saint John Chrysostom, for instance, boldly announced that Christians should receive the Royal Body of the Lord by forming a throne with their extended hands. On learning this, Pope Paul VI granted the bishops an *indult*, permission to deviate from Church law, to allow the laity to choose to receive Communion on their tongue or in their hands.

In the United States, this practice began around the time of the Second Vatican Council (1962–1965). This option was sometimes accompanied by and sometimes preceded by the institution of extraordinary ministers of Communion, laypeople trained to share the Body and Blood of Christ with the assembly and with those unable to attend Mass because of illness or age. The older practice of receiving Communion in the hands was reinstated to offer the baptized community the sacramental immediacy of the Body of Christ.

This practice illustrates how the Eucharist incorporates gestures and acts in some groups and not in others. It took no time at all for the U.S. laity to embrace the ancient practice of receiving Communion in their hands, but it didn't catch on so quickly in most other countries. Even to this day it's a custom many Catholic visitors to the United States, including future citizens, find surprising. After sufficient explanation, however, many of these men and women come to understand the tradition behind this link with the early Church.

With that in mind, it's interesting to note that Pope Benedict XVI asks those who receive the Eucharist from him to kneel and receive it on their tongues.

Veiled or gloved hands have been part of the Roman liturgy for centuries. Covered hands signal a respect and honor for that which is being touched. During pontifical ceremonies with a bishop, for instance, those who hold his crosier or the miter do so with veiled hands. Gloves are worn by altar servers during solemn celebrations of the Church year. A bishop wears gloves in the Latin Mass. In the secular world, men and women wear gloves on formal occasions. In some cultures, pallbearers wear gloves.

Liturgical law doesn't mention gloves, so common sense should guide us in this matter. If the gloves are worn as a sign of respect and honor, by all means wear them when receiving the Eucharist in your hands. But gloves that are more functional in nature (work gloves, medical gloves, and gloves that keep hands warm in cold weather) should be removed before receiving the Eucharist in the hands.

In the end, what is important is our mindfulness of and respect for the gift we are receiving. Reverence and respect must accompany this intimate and tactile encounter with Christ.

15. What should I do if I drop a consecrated host?

This question resonates with the profound sense of respect we humans are called to have for food in general. What is true for food that sustains our physical lives is also true of the food that sustains our spiritual lives: the Eucharist. It is with respect that we come forward to share in the Bread of Life and the cup of Eternal Salvation.

The *Tridentine Missal,* the Mass book from the Council of Trent (1545–1563), advised that if a consecrated host dropped out of someone's mouth or hand, the priest should pick up the host and cover the place where it fell with a linen cloth. At the end of the celebration, the priest was to return to the place where the host dropped, wash the area with water, dry the area with the linen cloth, and then reverently wash the cloth with which the area was dried. This extended ritual demonstrated a concern that not one particle of the host be trampled underfoot.

Since the Second Vatican Council (1962–1965), reverence for sharing the Body of Christ remains, but the new missal no longer contains lengthy procedures for washing the area where a host might fall. Instead, it is left to common sense and the respect of both the priest and the communicant for the Body of Christ. Therefore, if the host were to fall on the ground, the priest or the communicant should reverently pick it up and set it aside for later disposal by the priest. No other ritual cleaning is prescribed.

If the Precious Blood is spilled, wash the area with water, and then pour the water into the *sacrarium*, a special sink usually located in the sacristy that drains directly into the earth instead of through the sewage system.

Dropping or spilling at Communion should be a very rare occurrence, because the sharing of the host on the tongue or in the hand should be done slowly and deliberately as we remember that the One who feeds us died so we might live.

16. Is it permissible to dip the host into the chalice to receive the Precious Blood?

It depends who is dipping.

According to the 2002 English translation of the *General Instruction of the Roman Missal*, Communion may be shared from the cup in three ways:

1. The communicant drinks from the chalice.
2. The host is dipped into the chalice by the priest, deacon, or extraordinary minister and placed on the communicant's tongue.
3. The communicant uses a special straw, usually made of silver or gold, to sip from the chalice. The Latin name for the straw is *fistula*.

Option 1 is the most common way of receiving the Blood of Christ. The communicant decides whether to share Communion in this manner.

Option 2 is called *intinction*. The priest, deacon, or extraordinary minister dips the host into the chalice, soaks the host with the Blood of Christ, and reverently places it onto the communicant's tongue. Proponents of this option suggest that it necessitates less wine and less cleaning of purificators (cloths used to clean the chalice), it's more sanitary and, for a smaller community, demands fewer eucharistic ministers. Those opposed to this option say the command of Christ was to drink, and intinction isn't really drinking; in addition, intinction prevents people from receiving Communion in the hand and keeps those who can't drink alcohol from receiving the host.

Option 3 is rarely used, even in the Vatican. Certain groups like the *neocatechumenate,* a group within the Church whose members want the Church to return to the teachings of early Christianity, have experimented with this option. Some people have suggested that drinking with a fistula serves as more sanitary way of sharing the Cup of Salvation if each communicant has his or her own straw.

If option 2 is the practice at a parish, can *communicants* dip the host into the chalice? This has become a custom in many parishes around the United States, but the answer is no. First and most important, the *Roman Missal* makes no provision for this form of intinction. Second, because disease is commonly spread by the hands, one wonders whether many hands dipping into a chalice creates a greater risk than simply drinking from the cup and wiping the chalice rim with a purificator. Third, dipping the host for oneself limits the sign of receiving the Eucharist from another person.

Catechesis on sharing the chalice is a necessary part of encouraging the community to do as Christ asked us to do. Catechesis also informs the liturgical assembly about the customs and regulations of the Church to ensure that liturgy is celebrated beautifully and meaningfully.

17. Are the eucharistic prayers in the Latin Mass the same used in Masses celebrated in other languages?

As of July 7, 2007, the Roman rite of the Mass has two forms: *ordinary* and *extraordinary*. The ordinary form, called the *Novus Ordo*, comes from the Second Vatican Council (1962–1965). It was made official under Pope Paul VI. The second, now known as the extraordinary form or Tridentine Mass, is the 400-year-old Latin Mass from the Council of Trent (1545–1563). It was most recently updated in 1962 by Pope John XXIII.

In each of these forms, the ritual outline is very similar. However, the ordinary form has more room for adaptation than the extraordinary. The ordinary form, which has been used around the world since 1970, allows parishes to use the local language and add cultural expressions of praise and thanks to God. The ordinary form may also be celebrated in Latin if there is a pastoral need.

In the extraordinary form, on the other hand, rituals must be strictly adhered to. The options that do exist center on the level of solemnity or simplicity with which the rite is performed, for example, the use of incense or extra ministers such as deacons or subdeacons. The extraordinary form is always celebrated in Latin with the exception of the *Kyrie eleison,* in which we ask for the Lord's mercy. This is sung or recited in Greek.

In both forms, after the reading of the Scripture and the preaching, the focus shifts to the altar, on which bread and wine are placed. Over these gifts, the great prayer of thanksgiving is prayed. This prayer is called the *eucharistic prayer.*

In the ordinary form, the celebrant has a choice of thirteen eucharistic prayers. Eucharistic Prayer I (originally known as the Roman Canon), II, III, and IV are the most familiar of the prayers in the contemporary form. There are also two eucharistic prayers for reconciliation, three for Masses with children, and four for special occasions (also see question 32). In the ordinary form, these prayers are usually prayed in each parish's local language, but Latin may also be used.

The eucharistic prayer common to both forms of our present Roman rite is Eucharistic Prayer I (Roman Canon). In the extraordinary form, it's the only eucharistic prayer allowed, and it's always prayed in Latin. Some scholars date its roots to the fourth-century ministry of Saint Ambrose of Milan.

18. Can the Eucharist be celebrated outside of a church, for example, inside my home?

What an ironic question this is. The earliest celebrations of the Eucharist were held in the homes of the early Christians. In fact, house churches were not only buildings, but also ways of speaking about the early communities of faith: local households baptized in faith and confirmed in the Spirit celebrated the Lord's Supper together, sharing themselves and their resources.

As the centuries evolved and the Christian population grew, larger rooms were rented and later built to house the community gathering.

The term *church* is what we now call a building in which people worship. If we were to be accurate to historical development, we would most likely call the building the house or shelter for the Church because the Church is understood primarily as the baptized community living in faith and charity.

Throughout the centuries, these buildings have been the center in which the community gathers to celebrate the sacraments and the feasts and seasons of the liturgical year. One only need look at architecture books to see the various shapes and forms church buildings have taken. From Romanesque to Gothic, Baroque to Modern, church buildings seem to take the shape of the era and culture in which they are constructed. In turn, these buildings have shaped the rituals and religious imaginations of those who gather in them for prayer and celebration.

Unfortunately, because of changing demographics and the shortage of priests, many communities are consolidating and many buildings are being shut down and even destroyed. As a result, communities grow larger and places for liturgy do the same. Large communities can easily become impersonal and pastoral leadership increasingly difficult.

In recent years, especially in the United States, many large parishes are developing neighborhood communities in an attempt to subdivide into smaller faith-sharing units not unlike the original house-churches. These smaller communities gather for regular prayer and catechesis. The pastor of the parish occasionally attends their meetings and celebrates the Eucharist with them. This is a prime example of where and when the Eucharist is celebrated outside of a church building.

In other situations, the Eucharist has been celebrated outside the designated buildings. For instance, the Eucharist has been celebrated at cemeteries, in convention centers at religious-education congresses, on the backs of jeeps for troops at war, at nursing homes or hospitals, or in stadiums during papal visits. Clergy sometimes, but rarely, celebrate the Eucharist in places other than a church building when they are alone or on vacation. Some clergy celebrate Mass at homes with their families and friends at holidays or other family occasions.

However, local clergy cannot be available for celebrations of the Eucharist at family homes on any given day, especially on weekends. Church law restricts the number of Masses at which a priest may preside in a day. Masses at family homes, while permissible, are rarer now because of this limitation.

It's important to remember that, while the Eucharist may be celebrated outside of the church building, the celebration of other sacraments in other places is not always allowed. For instance, many diocesan bishops prohibit the celebration of marriages outside a designated church structure.

19. What type of vessels can be used during the consecration?

According to the 2002 *General Instruction of the Roman Missal*, the vessels used at eucharistic celebrations are to be fashioned with the best possible materials. This, of course, will depend on the economic state of each parish. If metals less precious than gold are used, the inside of the vessel should be gilded to prevent rust (paragraph 328). In the United States, nonmetal materials such as ebony or other hard woods that don't break or easily deteriorate may also be used (329).

Artists are free to create sacred vessels in the style and tradition of their local region as long as the vessels don't look like the kind used for regular meals (332).

Vessels used at Mass are to be treated with respect. The care, cleaning, and handling of these vessels demands mindfulness on the part of sacristans, Communion ministers, and clergy (327) to show respect and honor to the community that uses them. The sacredness of the vessels is a reflection of the beauty and nobility of the people who will use them to share the Eucharist of Christ's Body and Blood.

20. In my parish, the assembly doesn't kneel during the consecration. Is this normal or allowable?

Paragraph 43 of the Latin text of the 2002 *General Instruction of the Roman Missal (GIRM)* restates the ruling of the 1975 *GIRM*: The assembly stands during the eucharistic prayer, then genuflects with the presider after he shows them the consecrated host and chalice. In both editions of the *GIRM*, it was left up to the local bishops' conferences whether to follow that directive, and the United States conference amended it in the 1970s to say the assembly kneels at the conclusion of the *Sanctus* ("Holy, Holy, Holy") and remains kneeling until the conclusion of the eucharistic prayer, the Great Amen. People are excused from kneeling for reasons of health, lack of space, or other pastoral issues.

But because the 1975 *GIRM* directive to stand has been followed throughout most of the world, and because other areas of the liturgy were developing, many U.S. bishops and pastors thought the United States posture for the eucharistic prayer would eventually revert to the more universal directive. In anticipation of this, they encouraged standing and allowed church buildings to be constructed without kneelers.

In the July 2003 newsletter of the Bishops' Committee on the Liturgy, however, the U.S. bishops reaffirmed their 1975 ruling on kneeling. Since then, many parishes that formerly stood now kneel, and some do not. Some bishops have insisted the *GIRM* be followed, and others have not.

21. I understand Pope Benedict XVI allows the old Latin Mass to be celebrated at any parish. Is this true?

Yes, but with some conditions.

On July 7, 2007, Pope Benedict XVI legislated a change in Roman Church law. In two apostolic letters called *Motu Proprio Data* and *Summorum Pontificum: On the Use of the Roman Liturgy Prior to the Reform of 1970*, the pontiff outlined the legislation, encouraged the bishops to accept it, and assured them that their authority as leaders of their dioceses would in no way be curtailed by it.

The new legislation gives universal permission to all clergy who demonstrate competency in the Latin language to celebrate the Mass of the Council of Trent (1545–1563)—the Latin

Mass—without getting permission from their local bishops or superiors as long as certain guidelines are followed:

1. Individual priests may celebrate the Latin Mass privately, without a congregation present and without it being announced publicly. If other people happen to be there, they may attend also.
2. If a small group already devoted to the ancient rite asks a pastor to celebrate the Latin Mass, the pastor should honor their request. If he can't, the people should contact the bishop. If the bishop can't fulfill their request, he should ask the Vatican for assistance.
3. A bishop may assign certain parishes in his diocese to celebrate the Latin Mass.
4. In any parish, if there is a genuine need and request, the Latin Mass may be celebrated once on a weekend.
5. Priests and bishops may also celebrate the other sacramental rites of the Council of Trent: funeral rites, the Divine Office, and Liturgy of the Hours.

The response to the apostolic letters was mixed. Some sectors of the Roman Church are delighted that the Latin Mass, which had never been officially abolished, may now be used without barriers. They see an opportunity to unite communities that had become separated from the Roman Church because of the liturgical changes of the Second Vatican Council (1962–1965; see questions 33 and 34). They also see the ruling as a way to recover lost parts of our liturgical tradition, especially music, clerical apparel, and rituals of the past.

Other sectors interpret the ruling as a danger to the liturgical renewal of Vatican II because they believe it questions the authority of the local bishops and threatens the unity and integrity of parishes.

22. When are Catholics allowed to receive Communion in a non-Catholic church?

In 1993, John Paul II approved the Pontifical Council for Promoting Christian Unity's *Directory for the Application of Principles and Norms on Ecumenism*. This document outlined rules to guide ecumenical cooperation between baptized Christians of various denominations.

Roman Catholics are allowed to receive the Eucharist at Orthodox Churches even though these Churches are not directly connected to the Vatican. We believe these ancient Churches have common roots with the Roman Church and celebrate true sacraments. The Orthodox Churches, however, don't agree; therefore, Catholics should not receive the Eucharist in the Orthodox Churches until real unity is restored (paragraphs 122–128).

In cases of serious pastoral or personal necessity such as the danger of death or the dire inability to share the sacraments in the Catholic communion, Catholics may receive the sacraments from an Episcopalian priest who was ordained a Roman Catholic priest and then left the Catholic communion to join the Episcopal Church (132).

Non-Catholics may also join in Roman Catholic sacraments in certain circumstances such as closeness to death, sickness, or other pressing situations. In those circumstances, people who cannot participate in their own churches may receive

Catholic sacraments if they believe in Christ's Real Presence in the Eucharist, ask for the sacrament on their own, and understand what is taking place (130–131).

These situations occur regularly in hospitals and with hospital chaplains. When bringing the Eucharist to a sick or dying Catholic, a hospital chaplain may be asked by a non-Catholic person in the same room to share Communion. In this instance, the sacrament could be shared according to the norms of the directory.

Part III

THEOLOGICAL QUESTIONS

23. How important is the Eucharist?

On the night before Jesus died, "he took a loaf of bread, and when he had given thanks, he broke it and gave it to them, saying, 'This is my body, which is given for you. Do this in remembrance of me.' And he did the same with the cup after supper, saying, 'This cup that is poured out for you is the new covenant in my blood' " (Lk 22:19–20).

For two millennia, Christians have taken this command seriously. Eating and drinking the supper of the Lord, sharing in his Body and Blood, is at the heart of the Catholic tradition as Christian disciples. Many theologies of the Eucharist discuss this importance and honor the great promise of this sacrificial meal at which the hope and promise of eternal life are announced and anticipated.

In recent papal teachings, the eucharistic liturgy is called a *school*. At this school, we are formed as ambassadors of peace and reconciliation as a living sacrifice of praise. Gathering for the eucharistic liturgy, the community is formed and shaped by the Word of God proclaimed and preached. Inspired by the Word and nourished by the living Body and Blood of Christ, we are sent on a eucharistic mission, a mission that ultimately is demonstrated in lives of justice and charity.

The importance of the eucharistic school is brought forward in the tension of choosing between a culture of death and a culture of life. We are offered many choices of how to be human, how to live, and how to relate to others, the environment, and ourselves. In all these choices, we are schooled in values, some of which are contrary to the glory of God. Greed, hatred, division, instant gratification, and self-centeredness are valued by many even though they bring humanity to destruction and unhappiness. The eucharistic school offers us another set of values. It offers us the living Spirit so we may become what we share: the image and likeness of the One who loved us to the point of death on a cross.

Becoming the image of Christ is our destiny. By sharing the Eucharist with us, Jesus invites us to that destiny, offering us an alternative to a culture of death and leading us into a community of life in abundance.

24. Where does the word *Eucharist* come from?

The tradition about the night Jesus was betrayed tells how he took bread and wine and gave thanks to God (see Matthew 26:27). The word for "to give thanks" in the Greek version of the Gospels is *eucharistiein,* the foundation of the word *Eucharist.*

Today, as in the past, the word *Eucharist* can be used in several ways. First, it can be used to identify the entire ritual central to Catholic life, as in "attending weekly Eucharist."

Second, it can be used to speak of the great thanksgiving prayer. Thirteen eucharistic prayers are available to be prayed in the new liturgy. The central disposition of these prayers is to give thanks and praise to God for all the good gifts given to us in Christ and in the Holy Spirit (also see questions 17 and 32).

Third, we can use the word *Eucharist* to speak of the reserved sacrament itself. The Eucharist is reserved in a tabernacle and can be honored and worshiped in private devotion. Often the Eucharist is placed in a *monstrance*, a standing holder that allows the Eucharist to be viewed at special times of public prayer and adoration.

At the beginning of Christianity, other names were given to this essential gathering of Christians. The Acts of the Apostles calls it "the breaking of bread" (2:42). In 1 Corinthians 11:20, Saint Paul calls the gathering "the Lord's supper." Other earlier names for the gathering were the *agape,* "love feast," or the *koinonia,* "communion." Even the Greek word *mysterion* was used to designate the central gathering rituals for Christians. These terms did not endure, most likely because as Christianity grew, the commemoration of the commandment of the Lord was separated from the context of a community meal.

Current usage also includes the word *Mass.* This word, of later origin, most likely comes from the Latin word *missa,* "to be sent" or "it has been transmitted." Both are interesting translations. "To be sent" is the injunction given to the assembly to go out, like the Apostles, to do the work of God in the world. "It has been transmitted" could indicate another dimension of this sending forth: the dimension of God's grace communicated to us in the gift of the Body and Blood of Christ, received by us in the Holy Spirit so we can transmit it to the world.

To receive this gift, we must lift up our hearts to God in thanks and praise. While it's generally understood that it's our duty to praise God for all the wonderful works of creation and life, it's also our salvation to give thanks—*eucharistiein*. The early naming of our gathering becomes a spiritual clue to salvation in Christ: the grateful heart, full of wonderment and praise for the gift.

25. What is a eucharistic miracle?

This question can be answered in several ways. First, one may say that by the power of the Holy Spirit invoked by the priest during the eucharistic prayer, a eucharistic miracle happens: bread and wine are changed into the living Body and Blood of Christ. This is indeed miraculous. By faith, we believe the impossible is possible. The Spirit working in the Church brings about a change in the very substance of the bread and wine—something impossible to detect by science, something in the natural order that is unthinkable. And yet the presence of Christ under the appearances of bread and wine is something we cherish as real and is the very heart of our Catholic tradition.

Throughout the history of Catholicism, the experience of the Real Presence of Christ has also gone beyond the substantial presence that is the miracle of the Eucharist. For Catholics,

Christ is also truly present in the movements of history, in the proclamation of the Word of God, at moments of liturgical gatherings of the community, in the ministers of the Church, in the poor and disenfranchised, and in the depths of the human heart. The ubiquitous presences of Christ are unique ways of knowing God among us. Nevertheless, the eucharistic presence of Christ offers to people of faith a miraculous foretaste of the transformation of all creation that will happen one day—when God will be all in all.

The term *eucharistic miracle* is also used by Roman Catholics who claim something unusual has happened to a consecrated host, for example, that a host bleeds, appears as human flesh, or does not mold or decay for centuries. Some have also suggested that a consecrated host will fly from the priest's hands over the head of a communicant directly into the communicant's mouth. These phenomena are reported only in the Latin Church, not in the Eastern rite or Orthodox Churches. Their miraculous claims usually concern icons that exhibit similar happenings.

Throughout the centuries of Roman Catholicism, many theologians and church leaders have debated the validity of these phenomena. One great thinker, Saint Thomas Aquinas, responded to similar claims of his own day. He said that if such occurrences happen it is because they are allowed by God because the faith of the community is very weak and feeble. In strong faith, such occurrences would be meaningless and unnecessary. Aquinas was also clear that if blood did flow from a consecrated host, it was surely not the blood of Christ.

The official Church has always been very cautious about the claims of such phenomena. Such alleged phenomena may attract a certain strata of the Catholic population, but in the larger context of the Church's eucharistic theology these stories distract us from the essential mystery of faith: the simple gifts of bread and wine by Christ.

The eucharistic miracle can also be understood as the transformed lives of the community of believers who become one body, one Spirit, in Christ. Though many, though different, though of many races, languages, and ways of life, the Holy Spirit is called upon all those who share in the life-giving Bread and the Saving Cup. All are made new. All are made one. In such a transformation, the miracle of hope is anticipated: that all creation will be one, beyond injustice and death, and all will sing the praises of God, sharing in a peace beyond all understanding.

26. Is it more desirable to receive holy Communion with bread and wine than by bread alone?

To answer this question, let us go back to the story of the supper Jesus had with his disciples the night before he died. At that meal, he offered his friends both bread and wine. He told them to take and eat and take and drink. He then commanded them to do this in his memory (see Luke 22:19–20). The early Christians gathered for meals, and in doing so fulfilled Jesus' command by breaking bread and eating it, by pouring wine and drinking it. They kept the memory of Christ alive in the community and passed the living memory on to us.

Shortly after Christians began to grow in number, it became impossible to hold household meals at which the command of the Lord would be fulfilled. It became necessary to create other rituals performed not in the homes of Christians, but in larger public spaces. These rituals were not dining-room table meals of physical nourishment, but symbolic meals of spiritual nourishment. After listening to readings and preaching, a blessing prayer would be prayed by the designated leader over bread and wine that had been presented by the assembled community. Then the community would share in the ritual eating and drinking, partaking in the New Covenant of the Body and Blood of Christ.

As the centuries progressed, so did the rituals. The cup was no longer offered to the community for a variety of reasons, including the practicality of numbers, concerns for health and the spreading of disease, as well as the growing sense of the sacredness of the Eucharist and the unworthiness of the laity. Second, because of this feeling of sinful unworthiness, the laity no longer shared the Communion gift.

By the turn of the first millennium, the Western Church was celebrating the eucharistic rituals in such a way that only the clergy were receiving the sacramental gift. In response, at the fourth Lateran Council in 1215, the Western bishops made it law that Catholics must receive Communion at least once a year. If without good reason Catholics did not adhere to this once-yearly Communion, severe penalties would be incurred, including exclusion from the Church buildings and the refusal of a Catholic funeral and burial. That it was necessary to establish this practice, which became known as the *Easter duty*, shows how infrequently Catholics shared the Communion gift, either in the consecrated bread alone or with participation in the Cup of Salvation.

By the beginning of the twentieth century, the practice of

Communion began to change. Pope Pius X decreed an earlier age for first Communion, bringing it from the beginning of the teenage years to the age of reason, around seven years old. To encourage the community to share in the Communion gift, parishes around the world organized Communion Sundays for certain groups and societies.

But the greatest changes occurred after the Second Vatican Council (1962–1965). Not only was the assembly of Christians encouraged to share Communion at each liturgy in which they participated, but they were also once again given the option of sharing the Cup of Salvation, the Blood of the Lord. This was a renewal of the earliest practice and a fulfillment of the command of Christ.

During the centuries when the community was not offered the option of sharing in the Blood of Christ, the official Church made it clear in its teaching that receiving the Body alone constituted a full Communion. Even though the community did not participate in the actual drinking of the cup as commanded by the Lord, the sacramental Bread contained within it the fullness of grace of the Blood of Christ.

While this teaching still is held as Tradition, the option to receive the Blood of Christ must be taken seriously. Participation in the Blood of Christ by the actual sharing of the cup offers a fuller sacramental sign of Communion and engages the assembly in the actual eating and drinking the Lord commanded we do in his memory. While the sacramental grace may be the same even if one only shares in the Body of Christ, the fullness of the sacramental sign is greatly diminished if one chooses not to share in the Cup of Salvation.

27. What is transubstantiation?

At the beginning of the Christian community, preachers and poets created magnificent descriptions of the Eucharist using images from the Jewish Scriptures as well as from the surrounding folklores. As the Christian centuries moved on, especially in the ever-developing European monasteries and universities, the concern among theologians was to create definitions of what the Eucharist was and to describe the changes that occur when the words of the priest are spoken over the bread and wine.

By the mid-sixteenth century, the Council of Trent chose one such explanation to be the official language and theory by which to understand the Eucharist, the theory we now know as *transubstantiation*. This theory, founded in the philosophy of Aristotle and clarified by Saint Thomas Aquinas, seeks to explain without ambiguity that the Eucharist is a substantial change of bread and wine. The very substance—the "bread-ness" and the "wineness" of the gifts—is transformed. Even though it looks and tastes like bread and wine, it no longer is; only the physical attributes remain. Bread and wine are now something new: the Living Body and Blood of Christ (also see questions 28–31).

The explanation offered by the theory of transubstantiation is still helpful. The challenge lies in how to take this doctrine of the Real Presence of Christ and make it come alive in the hearts and lives of Christians through vibrant descriptions in creative preaching and catechesis.

28. Are the wine and bread in the Eucharist really changed into Christ's Blood and Body?

Yes. This is the mystery of faith, the promise of the doctrine of the Real Presence of Christ. The more we understand and experience this mystery, the more we understand and experience how much more we do *not* understand or experience.

If you found that sentence hard to follow, you have an idea of the depth of the mystery into which we are called to participate.

From the early days of Christianity, believers in Christ experienced the Crucified and Risen One as being with them. They were not alone in the struggles of living good lives, in facing temptations, or in facing judgment, martyrdom, and brutal death. They felt a tangible presence of Christ that offered encouragement, light, and direction to their lives. When the stories were told—the Word of God proclaimed—they knew something of the divine presence that sustained them. They were keenly aware of the presence of Christ also in the memory of the martyrs and heroes who had shed blood in testimony to their faith. In the stories and at the tombs of these holy men and women, Christ was known. As the community reached out in service to the poor—the least of the brothers and sisters—Christ was known as present among them.

Moreover, in a unique and splendid way, these early Christians also recognized Christ's presence at the gathering of the community, the proclaiming of the Word, the sharing of the memory of martyrs, and the serving of those in need. When they gathered for the meal, they remembered the great sacrifice of love demonstrated in the extreme by Christ. In the symphony of this gathering, Christ appeared in the breaking of the bread. He was recognizable.

Throughout the centuries, gatherings of Christians have continued to experience the mystery of this divine presence. It is a gift of the Incarnation, a gift of perceiving at the core of history a living Spirit who inspires the transformation of all creation so God can be all in all.

As consideration was given to this presence, special attention was focused on the bread and wine. How is such a bedazzling presence possible? It still looks like bread and wine, so how is it the living Body and Blood of Christ? Theologians debated various theories to explain this mystery, all the time knowing that such a mystery can never be fully put into a theoretical framework.

In the mid-sixteenth century, the Council of Trent made one of the theories official: *transubstantiation* (also see question 27). This theory basically says that by the working of the Spirit, the bread and wine placed on the altar becomes for us the living Body and Blood of Christ. This change occurs at the very substance of the bread and wine. While it still seems to the physical senses that nothing has happened, all is changed to the eyes of faith. This change of the bread and wine into the Real Presence of Christ becomes the beginning of the transformation and change the Spirit is bringing about in the community of faith, in humanity, in the whole of creation. The hope of the Eucharist is that as bread and wine are changed into the gift of the Living Christ, all will be changed one day, divinely transformed to the glory of God.

29. What is the biblical basis for saying the Eucharist is the actual Body and Blood of Christ rather than simply part of a remembrance ceremony?

Each of the Gospels of Matthew, Mark, and Luke tells a similar story of the supper Jesus had with his disciples the night before he died. In his first letter to the Corinthians, Saint Paul also passes on the tradition of that supper and Jesus' command to "do this in remembrance of me" (1 Corinthians 11:24). These passages form the biblical basis for the belief that the Eucharist is indeed the Body and Blood of Christ.

From the early centuries of the Christian Church, these biblical passages have inspired the eucharistic practices and beliefs of our Tradition. They inspired disciples of the early centuries to gather for meals, breaking bread and sharing the cup. After the more stylized rituals began to emerge, the narrative of the supper and the proclamation of the death of the Lord found their way into the central prayer of the liturgy, what we now call the *eucharistic prayer* (see question 32). Linked to these emerging practices was a central experience of the Risen One present in the midst of the assembly.

Sharing the Eucharist engendered a new sense of identity in the community: They were *becoming* the Body and Blood of Christ, sharing in the mystery they had *become* through baptism and the Holy Spirit. The question was, what happens to those who share in the Eucharist? Who are we becoming? Such a new identity brought them to become a living sacrifice of praise to God. This was illustrated in the community's outreach to others in need.

As the centuries passed, Christians began to ask other

questions: Are we doing a memorial service, or is this real participation in the Body and Blood of Christ? Do we take Jesus' words literally or figuratively? Such questions moved from the earlier interest of what the Body of Christ calls us to be toward identifying the substance of this bread and wine we are given.

In response to these questions, theologians crafted explanatory theories about what happens to the bread and wine. By the mid-sixteenth century one of these theories, transubstantiation, was decreed by the Council of Trent to be the true explanation (see question 27). This theory teaches that the words of Jesus (as recorded in the Gospels of Matthew, Mark, and Luke and in Saint Paul's letter to the Corinthians) mean that Christ intended to share with his sisters and brothers the living Body and Blood of his real and active presence through a change in the very substance of the bread and wine: It looks like bread and wine, but it is the Real Presence of the One who died and rose for us.

30. Is there a *specific* time during the consecration when the host becomes the Body of Jesus?

We believe that by the power of the words and actions of the Lord and by the power of the Holy Spirit, the bread and wine presented at the altar are changed into the living Body and Blood of Christ (also see questions 27–29).

Catholics believe in the Real Presence of Christ given to us by the Lord and that this holy presence begins at the moment of consecration. But when *is* the moment of consecration?

For many centuries, thinkers in the both the Western and

Eastern Churches have pondered this question. Some say it happens at the beginning of the sentence, "This is my body." Others say it happens at the conclusion of that sentence. Still others claim it happens during the entire sentence. The same theories were proposed about the consecration of the cup. From the Eastern Churches, the theory was raised that it wasn't the eucharistic narrative that was consecratory, but rather the prayer of invocation to the Holy Spirit known as the *epiclesis.*

These theories continue to be debated, but to what avail? Even the *Catechism of the Catholic Church* does not specify when the consecration happens (paragraphs 1375–1381). But knowing the precise moment it happens doesn't seem to be as important as simply knowing that it does—that by the close of the eucharistic prayer, the elements of bread and wine over which the prayer is prayed, are now, for us, the Body and Blood of Christ.

The *Catechism* is also clear that as long as it looks like, tastes like, and is recognizable as bread and wine, the gift of Christ is truly present among us. If the bread were to mold or the wine turn to vinegar, it would no longer be considered the sacramental gift of the Eucharist.

This belief in the Real Presence is why the Catholic Church reserves the Eucharist in a tabernacle. As the sacrament for the sick and the dying, the Eucharist is saved and cherished as *viaticum,* "food for a journey." The reserved sacrament also becomes a center for devotion and prayer for many Catholics. Recent Church documents on the Eucharist stress the value of meditative prayer in the presence of the Eucharist. The tabernacle is referred to by John Paul II as a "magnetic pole," attracting us to a deeper communion with Christ after the celebration of the Eucharist.

The mystery of faith, moreover, adds another dimension to our lives as Christians: transformation into Christ. Whether we share in communion at the liturgy or contemplate the Lord in the tabernacle, the loving call of the Spirit is to change our hearts. Specifically, when does that happen to us? One never knows for sure. But by participation in the mystery of faith, we are changed ever more deeply into the One whose Body and Blood we share.

---

31. How do you convincingly explain to a child that the Lord is *really* present in the Eucharist?

At the heart of our appreciation of the real and living presence of Christ in the Eucharist is the experience of a gift. By helping children appreciate the wonder of a gift in their human relationships, we can help them move toward appreciating the wonderful gift of the Eucharist.

In 2000 I wrote a book for first Communion candidates and their parents, *The Gift of the Eucharist* (Silver Burdett Ginn). The book begins by asking children to recount stories of receiving and giving a gift. Then it shares with the children the great gift of life they received at birth—their bodies, their senses, their families, their friends—all around them in creation.

The book then tells them we are created by God, the great gift giver. All life and all holiness are from such a loving and great God. At this point, the doctrine of God as creator and giver of life crowns a child's personal experience of gift. This is a leap of faith that children are ready to make.

Next, the book shares the Good News that God so loved the world he sent us the greatest gift of all: his Son (see John 3:16). Jesus lived our life. He spoke about God, invited us to a heavenly banquet, and taught us to live justly, share with the needy and the poor, and work for peace. Jesus gave us the gift of himself. The book connects all of this to the experience of gift giving.

Finally, the book says that on the night Jesus was betrayed, he gave us a final gift: Jesus gave us his life, his living Body and Blood. It looks like bread and wine, but it's a gift of Christ.

That is as far as anyone can go—child or adult. The mystery of the gift of Christ's presence, which begins at baptism and confirmation, is consummated at the eucharistic altar and shared as a gift to us over and over. It's a mystery we can only approach in faith, because we cannot really understand its depth. It's a gift of love, eternal and in the extreme.

The final message of the book is that what we *receive* as a gift, we are to *give* as a gift. In the end, the Real Presence of Christ in the Eucharist takes us over, and we are changed. Our lives become a real presence of Christ to others. As we are changed into Christ, God is glorified. And in giving ourselves away as a gift to others, God is thanked for all good gifts.

32. Why are there different forms of eucharistic prayers? Do they mean different things?

The 2002 version of the *Roman Missal* contains thirteen approved eucharistic prayers: Eucharistic Prayers I, II, III, IV; three Eucharistic Prayers for Masses With Children; two

Eucharistic Prayers for Reconciliation; and four Eucharistic Prayers for Various Needs and Occasions.

The *Roman Missal* of 1962 gives only one eucharistic prayer for the Tridentine or Latin Mass (now also known as the *Usus Antiquior*): the Roman Canon, which is now called Eucharistic Prayer I (*GIRM* 2002).

Eucharistic Prayer I has been in use in the Roman Church for many centuries. The word *canon* literally means "a list." The Roman Canon is basically a list of prayers or petitions, in the middle of which is a memorial of the Lord's Supper and the great works of salvation.

At the Second Vatican Council (1962–1965), it became clear that the riches of liturgical renewal would benefit from additional prayer forms retrieved from early Christian practice. When Christians gathered around their bishops in the beginning centuries of the Church, the bishops improvised the eucharistic prayers. Some of these prayers were recorded and attributed to great bishops like Saint Basil or Saint John Chrysostom.

Short of reestablishing this practice, which is strictly prohibited by liturgical law, the renewed books of the liturgy included other prayers to be prayed over the gifts of bread and wine. Rather than being a list of prayers and petitions, these new prayers were intended to be a more unified composition narrating more clearly the wonders of God and Christ in history. Some of the prayers, like Eucharistic Prayer IV, are written with their own beginning before the assembly sings the *Sanctus* ("Holy, Holy, Holy"). Others of these prayers were inspired by the prayers used at early eucharistic gatherings.

Included in these new prayers of the 2002 *Roman Missal*

is the invocation of the Holy Spirit over the bread and wine. This formal invocation, called an *epiclesis*, has been added to the thirteen new prayers. This was a radical shift of strong theological importance because there was no explicit mention of the Holy Spirit in earlier versions of Eucharistic Prayer I.

This addition signals a renewed direction in theology. Vatican II, convened by Pope John XXIII, had as one of its goals to be a new Pentecost for the Church, a time of renewal in the Spirit. For many centuries, the Holy Spirit was considered the forgotten person among the most holy Trinity. In fact, the Holy Spirit isn't mentioned in one of the most popular devotional prayers of the Roman Church, the Divine Praises, which is prayed at the conclusion of the Benediction of the Blessed Sacrament. By the decree of John XXIII, the Holy Spirit was added to this devotional prayer.

The Holy Spirit is the dynamic gift of the Father and the Son. Where the Holy Spirit moves, change happens. Mary conceives by the power of the Holy Spirit. Jesus is sent to his mission and into the desert by the Spirit. Jesus bequeaths the Spirit to his Apostles, and Pentecost sends them forth to all the nations.

The Spirit continues to work in the Church. In the thirteen eucharistic prayers, the accent on the Holy Spirit celebrates that in the power of God, bread and wine are changed into the Body and Blood of Christ—and so are we.

33. Do any religions besides the Catholic Church hold the same teaching regarding the Body and Blood of Christ?

Yes, other religions believe the Eucharist is a sharing in the living body and blood, soul and divinity of Christ.

In its ancient roots, this doctrine of Real Presence is held by the Orthodox Churches (Greek and Russian, for example). Eastern rite Churches already in full communion with the Roman Church also cherish this doctrine (see question 34).

After the Second Vatican Council (1962–1965), several groups displeased with the changes occurring in the Roman Church decided not to conform to the renewed vision of the council. One such group is the Society of Saint Pius X (SSPX). Although they are formally separated from the Roman Church in other areas of belief and practice, the leadership and members of SSPX believe the doctrine of Real Presence.

The phenomenon of SSPX leads then to a deeper understanding of what belief in the communion with Christ means. On the one hand, this doctrine is about belief in transubstantiation, the doctrine that the Eucharist is a living encounter with Christ's body, blood, soul, and divinity (see questions 27–31). On that the Roman Church, the Orthodox Churches, and SSPX agree.

On the other hand, the sharing in holy Communion also necessitates other dimensions of belief: a communion in the bonds of a shared faith, a common doctrine, a harmonious sacramental practice, and pastoral governance. These aspects of communion are essential for participation in the Eucharist. Without such resonance of belief and practice, true communion in Christ is not fully possible. It is in these other dimensions of belief that the Orthodox Churches and SSPX are not in harmony with the Roman Church. Therefore, even though they believe in the doctrine of transubstantiation, a shared Communion table is formally impossible at this time.

Work is being done to heal these divisions. Since Vatican II, commissions of Roman Catholic and Orthodox leaders and theologians have created opportunities of dialogue that have moved the communion between the Churches, so much so that public appearances of the pope with the patriarch of Constantinople have become more and more frequent.

In summer 2007, Pope Benedict XVI issued a change of the Roman law to allow more frequent celebration of the Latin Mass of 1962. It is the hope of Pope Benedict that a more frequent use of the Latin Mass and extraordinary forms of other sacramental rites will signal the openness of the Roman Church to SSPX and other groups of Catholics who are formally separated from the Roman communion. Ultimately, full communion in the Eucharist among all Christian churches would be a public and tangible sign of the unity Christ prayed for at supper the night before he died.

34. Do the Eastern Orthodox Churches believe the same thing about the Eucharist as the Western Church?

Yes. The theological explanations of the Eucharist may differ, but the core of belief is the same. Here is a list of our common beliefs (also see question 33):

- The gathered community is called by God in the name of Christ and baptized in the Holy Spirit. We are called the Church.
- The Church celebrates the divine liturgy as both an act of praise and thanks and a gift from God of abundant life.
- The Church gathers solemnly around the bishops, the designated leaders of the Church. In the absence of a bishop, the community gathers for Eucharist around a priest sent by the bishops to order the assembly and its liturgy.
- Sunday is the central day for gathering. It is the day when the paschal mystery of Christ is proclaimed in Word and sacrament.
- The Real Presence of Christ is communicated to us as gift and act of grace.
- Christ is present in the Word proclaimed, in the community of the baptized, in the presiding bishop or priest and, in a unique way, in the Eucharist.
- The eucharistic prayer is the central act of thanksgiving and praise. By the working of the Holy Spirit, during this prayer the offered bread and wine are changed into the living Body and Blood of Christ.
- The divine liturgy is at once a meal, a sacrificial memorial, and Christ's promise to prepare a place for us in the many mansions of God's dwelling.
- Participation in the Eucharist is vitally connected with participation in the communion of the Church. Without this wider communion, participation in the Eucharist loses meaning and can actually cause disruption in the community.
- As the community shares in the Eucharist, it is changed.

Many theologians who study liturgy and sacraments in both traditions claim that the Church is engaged in the transformation that leads to *divinization*, the transformation of the community into Christ's living body.

- As the Church, we're judged by our charity and justice toward others, especially the least of Christ's brothers and sisters.
- Charity and justice become the criteria for judging the authenticity of our liturgical activities. Such actions become the new worship called for by Christ. He was the first disciple of this new worship in spirit and in truth.
- In all of this, God's work of redemption in Christ is brought forth to completion. At the end of time, the consummation of the Eucharist will be known in an eternal banquet feast that people of every race, language, and culture will be invited to share.
- All creation will be transformed. God will be all in all.

35. I often hear the Eucharist referred to as the *community*. What does this mean?

The connection between the Eucharist and the community of believers goes back to the writings of Saint Paul. In his theology, the community—the Church—is the Body of Christ. He develops this theology in his first letter to the Corinthians.

In vivid language, he describes the Church as a human body. It has many interdependent parts, each working together in the body. These parts are in a communion—a harmony—so the body can operate smoothly and without inner disruption. If one part of the body suffers, all parts suffer.

Saint Paul uses this analogy to encourage the Corinthian community, which he sees as disjointed and lacking cohesion. He wants them to become whole in Christ, to become holy and one. He acknowledges that this lack of communion in the body is most clearly seen in the disruption that takes place when the community gathers for the Lord's Supper. He chastises them for this disruption and calls them to recognize their identity as the Body of Christ.

Here is where the connection between the Eucharist and the community of believers happens. For Saint Paul, the identity of community is to be found in the living presence of Christ, in the Spirit. As the baptized community, the Church becomes the Real Presence of Christ in the world. This presence is known in a unique fashion when the community gathers to celebrate the Lord's Supper, a sacred time of eating, drinking, sharing, and building up of the bonds of communion. The community becomes one body with many members interconnected in love to the glory of God. This love, *agape* in Greek, becomes the hallmark of the Body of Christ. Soon, the word *agape* is used to describe the meal as well as the very nature of the gift that is to vitalize the Church, the Body of Christ.

Some centuries later, a North African bishop named Augustine of Hippo (354–430) would take Saint Paul's insight and immortalize it with his own. By the time of Saint Augustine, the Lord's Supper was no longer a meal at a home where people ate and drank. It was now more of a ritual meal at which the local bishop presided in a more stylized manner much as we experience it in our own era. The assembly would come forward to share the gift of the eucharistic bread and wine. This vital connection between the eucharistic bread

and wine and the Church has been one of the great renewals
of the Second Vatican Council.

36. How did the Second Vatican Council change the way we celebrate and understand the Eucharist?

In the 1960s and 1970s, many members of the Catholic Church
noticed a lot of changes in the celebration of the Eucharist—
changes in practice and in perspective.

Let us begin with a few changes in practice. The Second
Vatican Council (1962–1965) called for a renewal of the
liturgical books, including their adaptation to the accents
and needs of the local cultures in which the liturgy would
be celebrated. This revolutionary move opened the door for
liturgical experimentation, some rich in tradition and some
superficial.

The council also called for a change in the reading of
Scripture during the Eucharist. Until that time, the Sunday
Mass obligation was considered fulfilled even if one attended
only the offertory, consecration, and Communion of the
priest. This minimalist understanding of participation did not
include attending to the reading of God's Word. Most likely,
this was the case because the readings were in Latin and the
preaching was concerned about moral and doctrinal issues,
not the Biblical texts.

This changed with Vatican II. With an eye to opening up
the richness of the Scriptures, the call for a renewed *Lectionary* produced one of the great treasures of the renewal. Now
the Liturgy of the Word is understood to be an essential part
of the weekly assembly. Attending to the Word, well read and

well preached, becomes the occasion for a rich renewal of the Catholic imagination. In understanding the Word, the symbols of the liturgy begin to speak more deeply to the heart.

Another change in practice is the use of the vernacular—the everyday local language of the people who celebrate the sacrament. This change allowed the culture to take root in the liturgy more deeply and enabled people to follow and understand the readings without effort. Such a change of practice had not happened in the Roman Church since the first early centuries of Christianity, when the liturgy shifted from Greek into the everyday language of the time: Latin.

These changes in practice were inspired by changes in perspective. The major change in perspective was the renewed understanding of what the documents call the "priesthood of the baptized." With the renewal of the adult catechumenate in 1972, the Roman Church was well on its way to a great change of perspective. The Church was no longer the bastion of the clerics; it was the communion of *all* the baptized, both laity and clergy, in a common and shared response to Christ.

This perspective created vast changes in local-church governance. Parish councils gained an important advisory voice. Finance councils of active laity are now mandated in each parish by canon law. The change of perspective that the Church is to be a sacrament to the world gives the laity a unique and important voice, a noble vocation in society. Organized and inspired by the clergy, the community is a symphony of many ministries and charisms. At a time of clergy shortage, in many parts of the world the laity are charged by bishops to manage the affairs of a local parish.

The call of the liturgical renewal to full, active, and conscious participation is a clear demonstration of one of the driving perspective changes of the council: that all the baptized members of the Body of Christ have been given the Holy Spirit so that the reign of God may appear on the earth.

37. Are the readings at the beginning of Mass more, less, or equal to the celebration of the Eucharist?

The *Novus Ordo*, or the ordinary form of the Roman rite, is celebrated in two major parts: the Liturgy of the Word and the Liturgy of the Eucharist. These parts complement each other in a balance of Word and sacrament.

In his 2004 apostolic letter *Mane Nobiscum Domine*, which inaugurated the Year of the Eucharist 2004–2005, John Paul II describes the complemental elements. Using the story of the two disciples on the road to Emmaus on the night of Easter Sunday, John Paul likens the two parts of the revised liturgy to their journey. First, Christ breaks open the Word for them, preparing their hearts with an interpretation of the Scriptures. Then they recognize Christ as they break bread. The Liturgy of the Word, proclaimed and preached well, allows time for silence and reflection on the wisdom offered. It becomes the necessary overture for the celebration of thanks and praise and the gift of the sign and sacrament to follow.

Parishes are called to take the Liturgy of the Word most seriously and to bring it to a new level of proclamation. John Paul II admonishes all involved, but especially preachers, to cherish the Word and preach it so the depths of the mysteries celebrated may be recognized and received into the burning hearts of Christians.

In this context, the Scripture readings are given a prominence they didn't have in the older form of the Roman rite. In the *Novus Ordo*, three readings and a psalm response are the center of the Sunday Liturgy of the Word. This new prominence allows a more thorough proclamation of the Scripture and invites Catholics to cherish the Scripture as the Word of God in which Christ is present and speaks to us.

The *Lectionary* used during the Sunday Liturgy of the Word is constructed around a three-year cycle; each cycle features different texts from the Old and New Testaments. Each cycle unfolds a Gospel of Matthew, Mark, or Luke, and the Gospel of John is interspersed throughout all cycles.

Liturgical renewal will best continue with a conscious effort to build up the scriptural literacy of the Catholic community. The Liturgy of the Word is a complement to the Liturgy of the Eucharist. They exist together and become a pattern of the Christian life: knowing Christ in Scripture and sacrament, becoming Christ's presence in word and deed.

38. How is the Eucharist related to the other sacraments?

The 1963 Constitution on the Sacred Liturgy (*Sacrosanctum Concilium*), the first document published by the Second Vatican Council, calls for a renewal of the liturgy for the sake of the renewal of the Church and of the world. The Tradition of the Church acknowledges in its theology and in its practice that central to its liturgical life is the celebration of the Eucharist. In this sense, the Eucharist is related to the other sacraments in the same way the hub is related to the spokes of a wheel.

The Eucharist is the third of the three sacraments of initiation; *baptism* and *confirmation* are the first two. In this traditional order, an initiate would become a member of the Church in water, oil, and then bread and wine, the four major sacramental elements. Because of the unique identity they offer a Christian, baptism and confirmation are nonrepeatable sacraments.

On the other hand, because of the ongoing nature of conversion for the Christian disciple, the Eucharist is repeated again and again at the command of Christ. Each time we eat and drink the Eucharist, we renew our membership in the Body of Christ. This repeatable sacrament of initiation is necessary because of the distractions and blindness that can so easily set into the hearts of believers. When we say amen to the Body and Blood of Christ, we are renewed in the covenant of baptism and anointed once again in the life of the Holy Spirit.

The Eucharist also celebrates the anticipation of the future banquet at which all creation will be lovingly one in singing the praises of God. Recent papal teachings have likened the celebration of the Eucharist to a school in which we learn again and again the lessons of the reign of God and the peace of Christ, thus hastening their arrival (see question 23).

As Christianity progressed, the community began to celebrate a second baptism we now know as the sacrament of *penance*. The history of this sacrament is rich in connecting with the Eucharist. Penance celebrates God's mercy and offers a unique opportunity to the Christian to be reconciled to God and to the Church, joining once again at the table of the Lord.

During the sacrament of the *anointing of the sick*, we ask

God to assist the sick person so he or she is joined to the community again at the Eucharist. The sick person, strengthened in faith by the holy oils and the laying on of hands, gives witness in the liturgical assembly to the power of God made manifest in human weakness.

The sacrament of *marriage*, often celebrated during the Eucharist, becomes the mirror of God's love for all people. The marriage of Christians in Christ is a sign of the divine marriage union Christ has with the Church. By having children, married couples sustain the Church with new members who bring the community into another generation of eucharistic life.

Finally, the sacrament of *holy orders* does just that: It *orders* the Church, its members, its theology, its strategies, and its tactics. Essential to the ministry of the ordained is the ordering of the liturgical life of the community, especially the Eucharist. By presiding at the celebration of the Eucharist, the bishop or priest, assisted at times by the deacon, gathers the community in baptismal renewal and in the joy of the Spirit, which sends us out to be the living liturgy to our neighbor, to the earth.

39. How can the Eucharist be "real" and "symbolic" at the same time?

At the very least, a *symbol* is an object, word, or image that stands for—represents—something else. A good example of this is a wedding ring. The ring is a symbol of the couple's love and commitment, but it's not the actual commitment. If something happens to the ring, the commitment isn't affected.

But sometimes a symbol can stand for something else and

be that something else at the same time. In this context, the Eucharist is a symbol of Christ's love as well as the actual Body and Blood of Christ. It's an experience that joins divinity and humanity, that joins us deeply with Christ in a communion of love. Thoughts and emotions blend and, in the end, the symbolic activity of the eucharistic liturgy becomes the real life of the Christian community in the Holy Spirit. Such a community becomes the living sacrament of Christ.

Part IV

PASTORAL QUESTIONS

40. Why doesn't the Church allow holy Communion for Catholics who have remarried without first receiving an annulment?

A divorced Catholic who has not remarried may receive the Eucharist; this question deals with Catholics who have divorced *and* remarried without first receiving an annulment.

If we examine the significance of the Eucharist, we are face to face with the mystery of participating in the Body of Christ. Catholic tradition holds that this participation is not a matter of private rules put together for the sake of the individual. Holy Communion is a sacrament of *unity* with the Church, an ancient community that has developed norms and mores through years of debate, dialogue, and experience. Participants sharing holy Communion become one body in Christ. The amen of one member of the body is the amen of the entire Church.

A significant part of these communal norms are the Church's teachings and regulations about the sacrament of marriage. The Church believes that, according to the instructions of Jesus and the early community, marriage is an unconditional covenant between a husband and a wife, at least one of whom is baptized, and can end only in death.

This covenant is held very seriously by the Church. But not all couples stay together. Over fifty percent of marriages break up, some for very serious reasons and some for not. Divorced persons often remarry outside of the Church but still wish to be part of the community and to share in the Eucharist. Nevertheless, the Church's official teaching is clear: to share the Eucharist while in violation of the covenant of marriage is to dishonor the Body of Christ.

The human pain and suffering the break-up of relationships can cause is not to be underestimated, and the official stance of not allowing divorced and remarried Catholics to receive Communion is not meant to add to that pain. It is meant, rather, as an invitation to honor and respect the serious nature of the sacrament of marriage. It is also an invitation to heal.

One of the ways the Church seeks to help heal divorced people is by annulment. Through written statements and conversations, the divorced person seeks to be reconciled with a broken marriage and to learn new ways of relating so he or she doesn't make the same mistakes again. Once the annulment is granted, a divorced person is free again to marry in the Church and to share in the Eucharist.

41. Can a baptized Catholic receive Communion even if he or she has never received official first Communion instructions?

In the first millennium of Christianity, baptism, confirmation, and Eucharist were inseparable. In the first several centuries, candidates for initiation were primarily adults. During a period of preparation called the *catechumenate,* adults were shaped and formed for a Christian way of life—and death, since martyrdom was a real option before the fourth century.

The formation process varied but always included the reading of Scripture, praying, introducing the community's lifestyle, and helping the poor and needy. The adult converts' children, servants, and slaves were also brought into the household of Christ. At the Easter Vigil, all were baptized and anointed in the Spirit, and they shared for the first time the Body and Blood of Christ. After initiation, a catechesis called *mystagogy* was offered to unveil the depth of the mysteries in which the neophytes now shared.

By the eighth century, the empire had become a Christian state, so most of the adults had been baptized and infants became the primary initiates. Baptism, confirmation, and Eucharist began to split in the Western Church. Infant mortality was high. Because baptism is essential for salvation, priests didn't want to put it off until the bishop's visit at the Easter Vigil, so priests began baptizing infants soon after their birth. Confirmation continued to take place at the Easter Vigil because of the importance of the bishop's role in confirmation.

At that time the Eucharist was still given to the infant at baptism, usually in the form of consecrated wine lest an infant reject the host. But by the twelfth century, Communion from the cup was prohibited and the liturgical community no longer shared in the drinking of the consecrated wine, so infants were no longer given Communion at their baptism.

With this change, the three once-united sacraments were now three distinct moments in the life of Western Christians, and the practice of first holy Communion began. The Eastern Churches of that era, now known as the Orthodox Churches, never made this split, and they continue to baptize, confirm, and give holy Communion on the day of Christian initiation. Only Roman Catholics have three separate rites.

Bishops and catechists continue to debate the correct age for confirmation and first holy Communion. For a time those sacraments were celebrated together, but Pope Pius X changed that ruling and allowed children to receive their first Communion at the age of reason, about seven years old. Confirmation is still a dangling issue.

In theory, as long as one is a baptized Roman Catholic in grace with God and the Church, one is able to receive Communion without official instruction. However, it's best if an adult who was baptized Roman Catholic as an infant but was never catechized presents himself or herself to the local parish leadership so the joy of sharing in Communion for the first time can be celebrated with the community.

42. How do I become an extraordinary minister of the Eucharist?

An extraordinary minister of the Eucharist (EME) is a baptized Roman Catholic who gives the Eucharist at Mass and who, in many parishes, visits the sick and the homebound in prayer and holy Communion.

Since the Second Vatican Council (1962–1965), baptized Catholics have been encouraged to share their gifts and talents with their parish communities. These gifts include proclaiming God's Word, visiting the sick, organizing works of charity and justice, singing and playing music, catechizing and evangelizing, preparing liturgy and prayer opportunities, assisting at eucharistic celebrations, and helping others discern their gifts. Parish leaders are charged with coordinating these gifts into songs of praise to God.

To become an EME, discernment of these gifts is the first step, followed by

- faith in the Real Presence of Christ in the Eucharist and in the community of faith;
- a heart willing to share Christ with others, sacramentally and in the service of human need;
- an ability to be present to people, especially to the sick and the homebound; and
- the time to do the work, and the willingness to commit to the duties.

Usually a person who has discerned the gifts for this ministry approaches a parish leader and asks to serve as an EME, but sometimes it happens the other way around. Formation and training include catechesis on the Eucharist and training in the practical skills necessary to share Communion at Mass and, if needed, with the sick and the homebound (see question 43).

Most bishops require the names of those to be commissioned as EMEs to be sent to them for approval. The EME is then formally presented to the community, usually within the context of a Sunday Eucharist. At this time, a special blessing ritual is prayed over the EME.

After discernment, formation, and practical training, the EME is commissioned to share the gift of the Eucharist. Faithful attention to the schedule and fulfillment of this ministry enrich the lives of those who have been given this gift of service.

43. Can an extraordinary minister of the Eucharist carry the Eucharist to sick people who wish to receive our Lord, or can only a priest do it?

Extraordinary ministers of the Eucharist (EME; see question 42) are encouraged by the Church to share Communion with the hospitalized and the homebound.

The book *Pastoral Care of the Sick: Rites of Anointing and Viaticum* contains prayers, readings, ritual patterns, and Church regulations for EMEs visiting the sick and sharing the Eucharist. Pastoral practice in North America offers two options for transporting the Eucharist from the parish to the sick person. First, at the close of the Communion rite of the Mass, EMEs approach the altar and are given a small, closed container of hosts, after which they're usually dismissed from the assembly to take Communion directly to the sick. Some parishes have the EMEs bring a parish bulletin or an audio recording of the homily to be shared with the sick person as well. Transporting Communion in this fashion is a necessary part of the ministry.

Some sick people cannot receive the Body of Christ, either because they cannot eat solid food or because they are allergic to the gluten in the consecrated bread. In these cases, the parish can provide a safely sealed container of the consecrated wine for the Communion of the sick. The EME must be especially cautious of the sacred cargo he or she is transporting. All semblance of rushing or casualness is to be avoided.

The practice of keeping Communion in an EME's home for practical reasons such as a sick call later in the week is forbidden by canon law without the express permission of the local bishop. If an unusual circumstance necessitates holding the Eucharist in a safe place for a time before it's shared with the sick, the EME should consult his or her pastor or the pastoral leader of the parish.

---

44. When priests give the "last rites" to a person who is unconscious or unable to swallow, how can that person share in the sacraments?

The sacrament now known as the *anointing of the sick* was known as *last rites* or *extreme unction* until 1972, when Pope Paul VI changed the name, significance, and meaning of the sacrament. Last rites had been prayed only when a person was near death; now the sacrament is celebrated as a strengthening and honoring of the sick. Even if death is not imminent, people who are seriously ill, preparing for operations, or struggling with mental illness or who are elderly and infirm can be anointed.

Many parishes have structured a ministry of care to visit the sick and the dying, and families are encouraged to request Communion and the anointing of the sick for people who are seriously ill or dying.

During the ritual of the anointing, the sacrament of penance is sometimes celebrated. Therefore, although Communion can be shared by an extraordinary minister of the Eucharist or a deacon as well as a priest, penance and the anointing of the sick may be celebrated only by a priest.

A patient who is unconscious is hard-pressed to participate in the anointing of the sick; however, if the priest can ascertain that if conscious, the patient would request the sacrament of his or her own volition, the priest may celebrate the anointing. Since an unconscious person or someone who cannot swallow can't fully participate in the action of eating or drinking, sacramental Communion would be impossible to share in such circumstances, and a spiritual communion prayer may be offered instead (see question 1).

Sacraments may be administered only to the living. If the priest isn't certain whether the person is close to death or has actually died, he celebrates the sacrament conditionally, meaning it is a sacrament only if the person hasn't died. If the priest is certain the person has died, he simply prays with those gathered.

45. Catholics have baptismal and confirmation sponsors. Why don't we have Communion sponsors?

The word *sponsor* comes from the Latin word that means "to pledge." To sponsor someone in societal terms means to vouch for them by one's own promise and pledge. Think of a country club. Many ask that any new member be sponsored by an existing member who can attest to the character of the new member lest the quality of the club diminish. A sponsor makes promises the new member must keep.

Another example is the sponsor chosen by someone who is recovering from addiction. In this case, a sponsor is someone to whom the neophyte can turn for assistance, support, and wisdom during the challenging road to recovery.

These examples are analogous to baptismal sponsors for both adults and infants in the present practice of the Catholic Church. In the adult-initiation rite, a candidate for baptism (catechumen) is required to have a sponsor. The first duty of the sponsor is to give witness to the good character of the catechumen at the rite of election. This public ritual, held forty days before Easter on the First Sunday of Lent, formally puts the catechumen forward as a worthy disciple. The sponsor attests that the Holy Spirit has been working in the catechumen and that he or she will be ready to become part of the Body of Christ at Easter. The sponsor makes a journey with the catechumen throughout the Lenten season and then stands with the catechumen in the waters of baptism, publicly acknowledging the confidence the sponsor has in the new member of the Church. The journey of the sponsor continues throughout the life of the newly baptized.

From ancient times, infants were required to have sponsors because they could not speak for themselves. By the end of the second century, a North African writer named Tertullian (155?–220?), who opposed the baptism of infants, warned parents and sponsors that if they made vows for the infant, they were responsible before God if the infant ever abandoned the way of Christian discipleship. Sponsors were accountable because they had made the promises.

These days, parents presenting their infants for baptism are told they are the first teachers of their children in the ways of faith. Baptismal sponsors, also known as *godparents*, are chosen to assist parents in this duty.

Later, a child or adolescent preparing for confirmation chooses a sponsor. In many cases, the candidate's baptismal sponsor serves in this role. The sponsor stands with a confirmation candidate in front of the bishop or his delegate and acknowledges the sincerity of the young person. While the sponsor does not make the vows for the candidate in this rite, the sponsor and candidate renew their baptismal vows together. The sponsor supports the candidate during the rite and into the future.

So why is there no sponsor at first holy Communion? In a way, there is. The baptismal sponsors, the parents and—if confirmation has preceded the first Eucharist—the confirmation sponsor join to support the first communicant in completing the sacraments of initiation. And while not formally called for by liturgical or canon law, sharing in holy Communion is always a sponsoring activity as we stand together at the great marriage banquet of the Lamb of God.

46. Is there a time when I should not take part in the Eucharist?

Before the Second Vatican Council (1962–1965), Roman Catholics around the world received the Eucharist much less frequently than they do now; in fact, they needed to be reminded to make their "Easter duty" (see question 26), the official requirement set forth nearly eight hundred years ago that at Easter each Catholic must confess his or her mortal sins to a priest and receive the Eucharist. To not follow this teaching was a mortal sin.

After Vatican II, things changed. The Constitution on the Sacred Liturgy (*Sacrosanctum Concilium*), the first document published by the Council, encourages frequent Communion on the part of the baptized and also permits the laity to receive Communion from the chalice (paragraph 55). This recommendation was responded to with great zest by the laity around the world. Now at each celebration of the Eucharist, nearly all participants come forward to share in the gift of the Lord's Body and Blood.

The *Catechism of the Catholic Church* states clearly that Catholics must prepare themselves before receiving the Lord's Body and Blood and that anyone who has committed a grave sin must go to reconciliation before receiving Communion (1385). Taking the lead from Saint Paul (1 Corinthians 11:27–29), Catholics are to examine their relationships— with family, neighbor, friend, enemy, planet, those who are in need, their own selves and, ultimately, with God— before sharing in the Body and Blood of Christ. If we discover that we have seriously violated the Body of Christ, we must allow ourselves to experience the overwhelming mercy of God and the renewal of our hearts and minds in the sacrament of reconciliation.

The sacrament of reconciliation is another chance at baptism. Baptism is the nonrepeatable sacrament. In early times, Christians who sinned after being initiated into the Body of Christ were considered to have cut themselves off from the Body, to have broken the communion. Gradually, the practice of a second baptism, known as reconciliation or penance, grew up in the Church. By the end of the first millennium, Catholics had the ongoing possibility of confessing serious sin to a priest as a mode of reentering the communion of the Body of Christ, so reconciliation is another baptism of sorts.

We still have that passage. When we find ourselves broken away from the Body of Christ by serious sin, the sacrament of reconciliation offers a healing grace. When we have a sincere and contrite heart, our sins are forgiven and we are again in communion with the Body of Christ.

So unless we've committed serious sin, we are warmly invited to share the Body and Blood of Christ at every Eucharist in which we participate.

47. Can a priest or bishop refuse to give someone Communion? Why or why not?

The short answer to this question is yes. According to *Code of Canon Law* 915, people who have been excommunicated, received an interdict, or who regularly commit grave sin may not receive Communion. Canon 916 adds that those who are aware of grave sin may not celebrate Mass or receive the

Eucharist without first going to reconciliation or promising to do so at the first opportunity.

Canon 915 is about decisions made by bishops, priests, and ministers of Communion. Canon 916 is about the internal decision of an individual person as to his or her worthiness to share in the sacrament.

In their June 18, 2004, publication "Catholics in Political Life," the United States bishops addressed the specific issue of denying Communion to Catholic politicians who publicly support legalized abortion. They left the interpretation of canon 915 up to each bishop. Because of this, different dioceses have different policies.

48. Can people with celiac disease or alcoholism take substitutes for the wheat host and wine?

This is becoming an increasingly important pastoral issue in many parts of the world. In some cases, food allergies are so toxic that even a bit of the allergen can lead to death.

Attention was drawn to this issue when a bishop refused a mother's request to allow her child to receive first Communion with a wafer made from rice. The bishop suggested the child receive Communion only from the cup. Not satisfied by this recommendation, the entire family joined a Christian denomination that allowed the use of rice wafers.

The Vatican has decreed that there must be at least some gluten in the host to make it valid bread for Communion and that men who have celiac disease should not be admitted to the priesthood because the priest must be able to eat and drink the Body and Blood of Christ.

So how much is *some* gluten? The Vatican was not specific. A group of United States Benedictine nuns took on the challenge of making a wheat host that would contain .01 percent gluten. Their recipe was approved by the Vatican in July 2003. Since that approval, the nuns have been amazed at the number of requests they receive for these low-gluten wafers.

Low-gluten hosts are usually purchased by the parish and consecrated at the same time as the gluten hosts, with the low-gluten hosts placed in a separate container. Communicants who cannot tolerate even the low-gluten hosts may choose to share only in the cup of Communion.

A similar situation arises with respect to the amount of alcohol in the consecrated wine. Some people are under the impression that alcoholic priests are allowed to drink regular grape juice at Mass instead of wine, but this isn't true. In July 2003, Pope Benedict XVI was Cardinal Joseph Ratzinger, prefect of the Congregation for the Doctrine of the Faith. He issued a letter ("The Use of Mustum and Low-Gluten Hosts at Mass") stating that priests who cannot drink wine must use *mustum*, a type of grape juice in which fermentation is allowed to start but is stopped while the alcohol content is still below the amount found in wine. But grape juice that contains no alcohol is not valid for use at Mass.

A priest who uses mustum simultaneously consecrates sacramental wine for the rest of the congregation.

49. For many years, when the priest said "The Lord be with you," we said, "And also with you." Now I understand the language is changing to "And with your spirit." Why the change?

The Second Vatican Council (1962–1965) required the liturgies of the Roman Church to be celebrated in local languages. The first round of translations from the Latin (late 1960s and 1970s) followed a set of guidelines that emphasized meaning rather than a strict translation of the words.

In May 2001, the Vatican congregation that regulates the liturgical books and rituals of the Roman Catholic Church published a document entitled On the Use of Vernacular Languages in the Publication of the Books of the Roman Liturgy (*Liturgiam Authenticam [LA]*). This document sets forth new rules and regulations for accurate translation of liturgical texts into local languages around the world. The local-language versions of the liturgical text must remain strictly aligned to the Latin original.

The Latin text for the greeting used during the Roman liturgy, "*Dominus vobiscum*," is currently translated to "The Lord be with you." This is a literal translation of the Latin and will stay the same. The response, "*Et cum spiritu tuo*," has been more literally translated to "And with your spirit." The current translation, "And also with you," isn't exact enough according to the standards of *LA*. The principles of *LA* will guide the entire translation of texts until new directives are issued by the Church.

In the new translation process, a Latin liturgical book is translated into a local language. The translation must be approved by the local bishops and then recognized by the Vatican as harmonious with the original Latin. This process will keep the unity of the Church's liturgy while allowing diversity of cultural expressions and languages.

50. Is the sacrament of the Eucharist celebrated the same way in all Roman Catholic churches around the world?

When I was taking my comprehensive examinations, the examiner said, "According to Church doctrine, Jesus Christ is both God and man." He paused, and then asked, "Please comment on the word *and*."

What makes Catholicism so rich is indeed the word *and*. Even the word *catholic*, which means "universal," offers a sense of the scope and riches of our faith. For instance, while other Christians may hold only Scripture as a place of revelation from God, we Catholics hold the Scripture and Tradition of the Church as a single fountain of God's revealing truth and love.

So the answer to this question is yes, it is the same, and no, it is not the same.

It is yes in that in Roman Catholic churches around the world, the eucharistic celebration of the ordinary form of the Mass is patterned in the same way: opening rites, Liturgy of the Word, preparation of the gifts, Liturgy of the Eucharist, and closing rites.

The answer is no because even though the general pattern is the same, when the sacramental liturgies of the Church were revised, the Second Vatican Council mandated that local churches from different cultures adapt the rites to speak in the accents of the people celebrating the Eucharist.

And then yes again, because in July 2007 Pope Benedict XVI confirmed the valid celebration of the Latin Mass, sometimes called the Tridentine Mass or extraordinary form. This form demands conformity of style and language: Latin language with regulations for the liturgy that offer no options.

And then no again, because even in the Latin Mass the quality of music, participation, familiarity of the celebrant with Latin, and regulations vary. Also, the Latin Mass has different levels of solemnity that change the tone of the ritual.

And then yes again, because the climax of the eucharistic celebration in either form is the communion of God's people in the living Body and Blood of Christ. The sharing of Communion is encouraged of all the faithful who celebrate the Eucharist.

And then no again, because some share Communion on their knees and others stand; some receive it on their tongues and others in their hands; some share the consecrated bread only and some the consecrated bread and cup.

And, finally, yes again, because the aim of all eucharistic celebrations of the Roman Catholic Church, regardless of the form, is to give glory to God. God's glory is best expressed when the local parishes work for peace and justice in the world. The goal of all celebrations of the Lord's Supper is to transform the community into a living sacrifice of praise. The sacrifice that ultimately is pleasing to God is that of Christ, whose mercy to us causes us to become merciful to each other.

SOURCES

United States Conference of Catholic Bishops

The following documents are published by the United States Conference of Catholic Bishops, USCCB Publishing, 3211 Fourth Street, NE, Washington, DC 20017-1194; 800-235-8722 or 202-722-8716. They are also available online at www.usccb.org.

Catechism of the Catholic Church, English translation, second edition, © 1994, 1997, 2000. United States Catholic Conference—Libreria Editrice Vaticana. www.usccb.org/catechism/text.

"Catholics in Political Life." Task Force on Catholic Bishops and Catholic Politicians. © 2004. www.usccb.org/bishops/catholicsinpoliticallife.shtml.

"Clarification on Posture of the Faithful Following Individual Reception of Holy Communion." Bishops' Committee on the Liturgy *Newsletter,* July 2003. www.usccb.org/liturgy/innews/703.shtml

On the Use of Vernacular Languages in the Publication of the Books of the Roman Liturgy *(Liturgiam Authenticam).* Congregation for Divine Worship and the Discipline of the Sacraments. © 2001. www.usccb.org/liturgy/missalformation/index.shtml; www.vatican.va

Roman Missal

General Instruction of the Roman Missal (Third Typical Edition)
© 2002, International Committee on English in the Liturgy,
Inc.; including adaptations for the Dioceses of the United
States of America © 2003. www.usccb.org/liturgy/current/
revmissalisromanien.shtml

A Commentary on the General Instruction of the Roman Missal.
Edited by Edward Foley, Nathan D. Mitchell, and Joanne M.
Pierce. Collegeville, MN: Liturgical Press, © 2007 by Order of
St. Benedict. www.litpress.org

1962 Order of the Mass [Latin Mass]. Available online only: www.
sacred-texts.com/chr/lmass/ord.htm

Vatican

The following documents are published by Libreria Editrice Vaticana,
Via della Posta s/n, 00120 Vatican City. They are also available
online at www.vatican.va/roman_curia/institutions_connected/
lev/index.htm:

Directory for the Application of Principles and Norms on Ecumenism.
Pontifical Council for Promoting Christian Unity. © 1993.

Mane Nobiscum Domine (To the Bishops, Clergy and Faithful
for the Year of the Eucharist, October 2004–October 2005).
© 2004.

Constitution on the Sacred Liturgy (*Sacrosanctum Concilium*)
© 1963.

Summorum Pontificum: On the Use of the Roman Liturgy
Prior to the Reform of 1970. © 2007. www.usccb.org/liturgy/
bclnewsletterjune07.pdf

Canon Law

Code of Canon Law: Latin-English Edition. Washington, DC: Canon Law Society of America, © 1983. www.vatican.va/archive/eng1104/_index.htm

New Commentary on the Code of Canon Law. Canon Law Society of America, edited by John P. Beal, James A. Coriden, and Thomas J. Green. New York: Paulist Press, © 2000. www.paulistpress.com

Miscellaneous

Book of Blessings. Collegeville, MN: Liturgical Press, © 1989 by Order of St. Benedict. www.litpress.org

The Gift of the Eucharist by Richard Fragomeni. River, NJ: Silver Burdett Ginn, © 2000. www.rclweb.com

Pastoral Care of the Sick: Rites of Anointing and Viaticum. Totowa, NJ: Catholic Book Publishing Co., © 1999. www.catholicbookpublishing.com

Visits to Jesus and Mary by Saint Alphonsus Liguori, Joseph Nolen, C.Ss.R., editor. Liguori, MO: Liguori Publications, © 2006. www.liguori.org

ACKNOWLEDGMENTS

I thank Fr. Mathew Kessler, C.Ss.R., president and publisher of Liguori Publications, for his encouragement and assistance in bringing this book to publication. I also thank my 2008 summer-school students from the music and liturgy graduate program at Saint Joseph's College, Rensselaer, Indiana. Their insights and approach to many of these questions inspired my own thinking. To Professor David N. Power, a special word of thanks for showing me ways of thinking about the Eucharist. And to Joseph Vuci, Jr., who keeps asking good questions from the pews.